Faith Renewed
By Courtland Morrison

Printed in the United States of America

CA Morrison Publishing

ISBN 978-0-9996128-4-2

www.courtlandmorrison.com

Acknowledgments

First, I thank my Father in heaven for granting me this talent.

My parents, my brother, and my entire family; thank you for your continued love and support.

To all my friends and military family, thank you all for supporting my writing career and for giving me a chance to share with you my unique blessing!!

Tamyara Brown LaToya Murchison, and Erica Stillwell; thank you for your contributions to this book. I appreciate each of you

Books by Courtland

First Steps

My Path

My Thoughts

Perception is key

Perception is key. My back is against the wind.

My eye is on the prize.

Yet I seek his grace and mercy; the solitude of the

Lord is truly divine.

I feel the wonderments of the climate which is the

physical presence all around me

Standing like a soldier in the army of the Lord

I am so grateful Jesus Christ died for my sins and

others that we might live and honor and worship

him as the true and living God

he is I stand with my back against the wind.

My eye on the prize

For I can see what blessings he holds for me, what

love cherishes me, and what faith brings me

My savior, the Lord of lords and king of kings, the

alpha and the omega, the beginning and the end

Jesus Christ strengthens me always

That standing wind are his angels in the physical

protecting us spiritually

yet my eyes are looking to the heavens for the

trumpet to sound to tell us to come home.

That is why I stand like a soldier in the army of the

Lord.

Courtland Morrison

Enough for Me

Verbal expressions monumental convictions
is what we share   pains of our heart.
Empathy of our soul from the darkest of places to
the brightest of lights on heaven or earth.
The walk thru the mountain tops to the valley lows
He is always with us. Yet just like footsteps on a
beach, and comfort us in front of our enemies.
He is our Lord and Savior. Jesus Christ is there.
He knows our wants, yet he knows our needs; he
blessed us always with faith to convene in him.
So, do not stress nor cry; he has seen the struggle
and pain.
"You have never been just enough but more than
enough for Me."
For he has already covered you and yours with
blessings beyond what the eye can see

Courtland Morrison

He is working on me!

A one of one masterpiece, he
sculpts and sharpens turn by turn
He breathes new air into my
lungs and adds fire to my soul
Each step measured not one
more not one less
Day by day, minute by minute, second by second,
He is working on me!
Those moments as time is crafted, he is making a
woman of spirituality, beauty, and intellect
A wife to a man, mother to her child, queen of her
household for she is embodied by God who has
made her, entrusted her, and brings her soul
Day by day minute by minute second by second
He is working on me and preparing me for his
salvation
Lord, I give you the glory
O how I worship thee and love you so
Courtland Morrison

Kingdoms Light

Whatever the light touches is our kingdom

Yet the rise of the sun, duskiness of the moon

Mine eyes have seen the glory.

This glory to see the expectations of distance.

Yet that light the iniquity of the world.

The light of the night.

Light of the day.

The embrace that protrudes from the darkness.

Whatever the light touches is our kingdom.

Kingdom of royalty,

Kingdom of our father,

The Kingdom of God.

Courtland Morrison

Why

Why are social justice workers called animals? If
they represent a specific group? Why is there a
double standard when doing the same work?
Why am I watched so aggressively when I enter a
store?   Why am I followed when driving a
particular model of car? Why am I taught at a
certain age to conduct myself when entering acting
with law enforcement? Why must the media shame
me in the court of public opinion?
Why am I looked down upon? Why is the color of
my skin a problem? Why can't you look at me for
the content of my character? Why I am thought to
be nefarious, cruel, an imminent threat
Why do these questions have to be asked over and
over
WHY??????
Courtland Morrison

Compositions

Written compositions, narrative expressions

Conveyance of words from my heart

One pen to one pad the sketch begins

Combination of words a foreshadow of

my thought process

A combining of ideals to project imagery of the

mind

A projection of wordplay that provokes mentality of

those around me

Compositions

An expression of my ideas and opinions

in written form

A delicate balance between words and emotions

Continual thoughts, expressing verbiage

The essence of words and emotions

A lover's quarrel brought to life

Compositions

My love of words

Brought to life

Courtland Morrison

Faith, Fear & I

Faith and I took a walk towards victory,

but fear intervened.

Fear reminded me of the losses, the

anxieties and hurts.

Fear seemed realistic, and so like any soul

wandering, I pulled towards fear.

I validated its lies because it seemed like the truth.

Faith seemed like a fantasy, and a dream deferred.

Fear spoke about what I could see in the eyes of me.

Faith fought for me in an intense

battle to heal the hurt in me.

Fear battled Faith because she had a hold of me.

Faith spoke into me and affirmed

even I turned away from it.

Faith wanted me to see the heavens

even in the storm.

They confused me, I can admit.

I sat in my room crying, pleading for a resolution of

which was valid.

Faith sat next to me, reciting God's words, blessing
my soul.
It erased all the sorrows instilled, or an exact time
for a woman lost.
Faith remained, and fear escaped.
Faith is love, and even though it is not immediate, it
never quits.
By Tamyara Brown

Resolutions

My resolution of mind is the gateway to my soul

Intemperance of life, the joys of happiness

I set to acquire

Expressions of thought, the loneliness of

wisdom is true

Ideas I see to bare, excess of love passion of self-

cured over my lifetime

The dogma of faint, a standard to achieve

Verbal illusionists' allegory of the mind

Cognizant institutions I sole to achieve

Conscription with a right hand, I dare to fight with

Awkward justice of the left that gleans in the light

True allegiance of the self-righteous, My

momentous feel

True love of self is my mind

Resolute thought is the status that I will achieve

Love of my mind, body, and soul

Resolutions

Courtland Morrison

My Roots

The strength of my soul can be traced to my roots

The roots of life, the roots of my soul Africa

The great continent that birthed mankind

My roots are priceless in value

My roots are in high demand

From the diamonds, gold, animals

My roots in Africa are in constant reverence

My roots from the people

My roots the knowledge base for all humanity

My roots the soliloquy of time

My roots a legacy defined

Courtland Morrison

My Depression

I see darkness in the air, smoke all
    around me
My world is of fire and lava
Death and destruction are my worlds
Terror consumes me

Light of the day brings tears to my
    eyes
I have been forsaken for futility
There are no rainbows or clear
    cloudless skies

I only see pain, violence, and unrest
The love is gone, but anger is ever-
    present
My mind is tormented   evil is like
    my best friend

Fire comes out my mouth; eyes are
    colored   red like a demon
Hate and grit filled my soul

Forgiveness is null and void

My depression, my mind, my psyche
My mental anguish has me at a loss
My depression
Courtland Morrison

The Conversation

He killed it. A message he delivered but will the
conversation ever start or begin
Will that conversation ever be acknowledged will it
ever be in mid-sentence
Will it be like the usual suspects and be deflected
and misinterpreted from the truth
What must happen what must be done for this
message to be brought to the forefront
Time and time again it brought up, yet the same
protocol is being used again
A stain of deceit, a point of rage
I feel no solution is possible
Yet I must keep my faith in the most-high
Injustice and systemic discrimination are a
Dagger in our country's life
This conversation must not start but be continual
until we are all united
That Dr. King so eloquently said "Judge me by the
content of my character rather than by the color of
my skin."
Courtland Morrison

I shine

I shine I thrive I innovate you
set my mind ablaze yet your heart is divine
you set me free to breathe
I feel the consulate of your mind, which brings
respect, peace, and love
write with passion penmanship, is boldness set my
mind free
from the pain of the world.
Free from the hands of the angered young man or
the cries of the lonely girl.
Lost to the concept of reality television,
yet mere talents are hidden to hold on this side of
the in-crowd
roller coaster ride has risen, and yet they remain
silent.
Instead of letting their light shine or unmasked the
skills within that have so far been
blinded. talk to me
Talk to me and see the deeply divine glory
Natural and powerful it burns hotter than the surface
of the sun yet colder than the arctic circle

Taller than the Himalayas it is my profound voice
that booms and shakes the ground
makes nature obedient yet calms me like summer
breeze coming off the ocean
young man young woman do not be troubled for
your true self is not of this world
show your strength and intellectual ability for the
concept of reality is happiness in
yourself
Love in yourself; success is in your hands
So, do not let another define your wealth; and do
not be fooled by their games
Their body language tells a lie because their
pockets do not say the same.
Yet our enemies will be our footstools, their pain
our grace.
For they had two when it came down to it, yet us
real ones keep our face...
The evil knows not what they afford. People give
me desire to push through the most turbulent times

The love of thine self-molds me, shapes me,
provokes me an intuition of fire that glows upon my
enemy's.
I am not fooled but delighted in being to speak with
the absence of profane and explicitly Segregate my
words to a few.
Give glory to the highest show the faith of walking
is not seeing is the most I need.
For I need thee oh Lord for in you, I trust and
believe.
While the enemy seeks to devour, your Love God
is my safety, my soul you keep.
I will press toward the mark for chosen
That I shall stand the test and real the harvest of
many blessings bestowed upon me from the most
high.
The blessings he gives are so many I bow down on
my knees to give him the most praise
Knowing he gave me shelter, food, clothing, and
ability to breathe in I am forever grateful

I know when I am down, never to look around for
the angels surround me to protect me for no weapon
formed against me shall prosper.
...and any tongue rising against me in judgment
shall be condemned.
For they boast and think highly of themselves, still
they will never sit higher than him.
Poses the power, orchestrate the hours, and still
have time to provide his grace like him
For he is the Lord of lords and King of kings
The alpha and the Omega the beginning and the
end.
He is the light that all shall see when the trumpet
sounds.
Oh, what a feeling of joy.
Courtland Morrison & Erica Stillwell

I initiate my mind

I initiate my mind to the highest turn of time I
gravitate pass the sun to the far etches of the
universe
The stars shine poignantly and glean my mind
My steps are ordered and protracted
One time and one approach
The glow of a presence all around
I glide, I slide, I walk
A surreal sense of touch, sight, and smell
The glimmer of knowledge misting over me
The distance of mountains in my quest to go over
Yet the wakes of the oceans to cross
These sights, my steps are being ushered
His presence around me
I am truly blessed
His vision for me defined
I initiate my mind
Courtland Morrison

My Husband

My husband the center of my world

My soul mate the king of my castle

My love for him cannot be described

He is the father to our children

He is the honey to my bee

He is the protector of my castle

His daughters emulate him

My husband is a God-fearing man

He instilled the presence of my savior

In all he did

My husband, my soulmate, my king,

My lover, my best friend

I look in the sky and know he is watching down on

my daughters and me

For the Lord knew it was your time to come home

I have so many memories, but I do not want to let

you go

It has been 15 years since you left, but your spirit

Transcends time

My husband I will continue to honor you

I will keep you in my spirit

I will keep your legacy and name sacred

Most of all I will love you and cannot wait to see

you again

My husband

Courtland Morrison

Lord orders my steps

The Lord orders my steps meticulously

His planning is beyond my knowledge for he is

forever wise

I crawl, walk, and run

His guidance is prudent

His resolve unmistakable

I look to my left and my right, yet I see no one

In my spiritual sense, I am protected by thousands

of Gods anointed angels

I must learn to use and be adept to my spiritual eye

That eye is of the Lord that

Helps me vision continually

Love for my enemy said than done

My Lord's blessings and omnipotence rule of

Judgment in what drives me to take heed to

Those ordered steps made for me

Courtland Morrison

In my mind's eye

I see a circumference of time

Meticulous attention yet authentic in detail

Archaic prints absolute in structure

Centrifuge of the mind

Minute quality implied connections

Perpetually vision of the spirited eye

Distinctive collaborations

Solitude of growth

Authenticity of my life

In my mind's eye

Reverence is my Lord before me

I promise and drop to my knees

To worship thee

The lord god

Is in my mind's eye

Courtland Morrison

Kisses

I am weak for his lips on my lips

I become intoxicated and drunk off his kisses

What possesses the universe to give me a gift of a

man like that

To erase away sadness

To spark a fire inside of me

His kisses are magically delicious

He is the soul stirrer and when my emotions

Are all over the place he is calm?

All with one simple kiss

You provide my life with lips on your lips

I am entrenched and magnified with the softness of

your kisses

The universe was set in a pattern like Orion's belt to

meet a woman like you

Your sweet kisses and soft touch

Keeps me in sacred trust with you

I give you my heart for you have the key to my soul

Your kisses and beautiful eyes keep me mesmerized

On you forever

Tamyara Brown & Courtland Morrison

My Skin

My anger grows, and my trust keeps

slowly going away

I assume, and I know I have a target marked on my

back. Simply because I am black I have melanin in

my skin, which gives me a more robust skin tone.

I am looked down upon, and yet my eyes just want

peace, justice, and tranquility.

My skin this coating of brown has been a demon

I am one to be feared, one to be disrespected,

never to be trusted

Anger, resentment, jealousy is a

reoccurring post about me

Fear the black man he will destroy your community

Fear the black man he will disgrace

all you hold sacred

Fear the black man because he is evil

So much anger and it comes and goes

So much resentment how do I displace it

So much hatred and injustice it swirls and swirls

So much racism that my blood boils

Courtland Morrison

Faith Talk to me, Please

Faith talk to me, please

Take the lead and give me strength

Renew me now I am drowning fast

I am clashing with all that I see

These two pandemics are leading me towards fear

Faith talk to me, please

I am leaning on you because the tests of the world

have shaken my beliefs.

Lead me to God and help me hear his answers.

Faith talk to me please and clear all the negative

talk fear has fed me

Remove the barriers between God and me

Let me kneel and pray

Remind me of his goodness and grace

Faith talk to me, please

Tamyara Brown

My Ascension to Christ

My ascension, my path the growth to eternity

I balance my thoughts of fallacy and modesty

Implicit and dexterity from the words by

the direction of my hand

I dedicate my tongue as the words recede in my

mouth

The letters that form words are the tools of my

profession

The decree of my craft comes from the

Lord who sits on a crown so high

We all must kneel to worship him

He all is seeing, all-knowing, he is the

Beacon of the world on a place covered by

Darkness

Our savior's greatest gifts eternal life and love

If only you speak from your heart and profess with

You tongue he will forgive you of your sins

Such a gift, a pleasure a thought so defined

Courtland Morrison

Look to My God in Prayer

Many thoughts to write Many times to convey

I got to my Lord in prayer I kneel on sanctified

ground

For the Messiah is in front of me I look up to him,

and he says Come to me my child

We walk and talk He shows me life and says you

Have grown from a child to a man

A man of valor, a man of courage, and most

importantly a man of faith and humbled

I am humbled but at the same time, grateful. I

worship thee

My faith, my prayers My faith renewed I look to my

God in Prayer

Courtland Morrison

I Seek the Lord

I seek the Lord for he is the light of the world

For his very being touches all our souls

That might that touch gives me joy

Gives me oxygen to breathe

Gives me empathy to love my neighbor

I seek my Lord for he directs my pathways

He knows the valleys and cliffs

He is the shepherd that moves his flock

I seek and cherish   my lord

For I am nothing without him

He is my everything

Lord you are my God, king of kings Lord of Lords

Jesus Christ the Messiah

My God, my king the one I seek

The one I worship

My Lord I seek you always

Courtland Morrison

Speak to My Heart

Speak to my heart Lord I can
fill myself slipping away.
I try, and I try, but it becomes harder
with the passing of each day.
Speak to my heart Lord because
of you, I have made it through the day.
Speak to my heart Lord as your light
shines bright, so I do not get lost along the way.
Speak to my heart when at night all
I can do is just cry.
Speak to my heart Lord because
I know it not my time to die.
Speak to my heart Lord speak to my heart as the
morning begins and gives me the strength to face
the world on this brand new
LaToya Murchison

Safe in His Arms

Safe in his arms is
where I desire to be.
Safe in his arms how
he will protect me.
Safe in his arms is where
he created a new heart in me.
Safe in his arms is
where true love will find me.
Safe in his arms is where
he supplies all my needs.
Safe in his arms is where
you will always find me.

LaToya Murchison

About the Author

Courtland Morrison was born in Texas and raised in North Carolina. He developed a hobby for writing poetry in middle school. Courtland joined the Army National Guard and served honorably with 2 combat tours to Iraq. While deployed he would write for fellow soldiers to help cope with combat and stress associated with it. He graduated from DeVry University in 2016 with a B.S. in Technical Management. He just recently graduated from Keller university DeVry's graduate school. He earned his MBA in Business Administration with a concentration in Global Supply Chain Management. His goal has always been to publish his poetry. Courtland has been told he is a gifted writer.

www.ingramcontent.com/pod-product-compliance
Lightning Source LLC
Chambersburg PA
CBHW020144150626
46552CB00021B/1647